THE FESTIVAL OF ART

Copyright © 1971 The Tree House
Library of Congress Catalog Card No. 79-135224
International Standard Book No. 0-8066-1107-3

Manufactured in the United States of America

The Festival of Art

By Gerard A. Pottebaum   **Illustrated by Ken Roberts**

Augsburg Publishing House
Minneapolis, Minnesota

One auburn afternoon a famous artist gathered

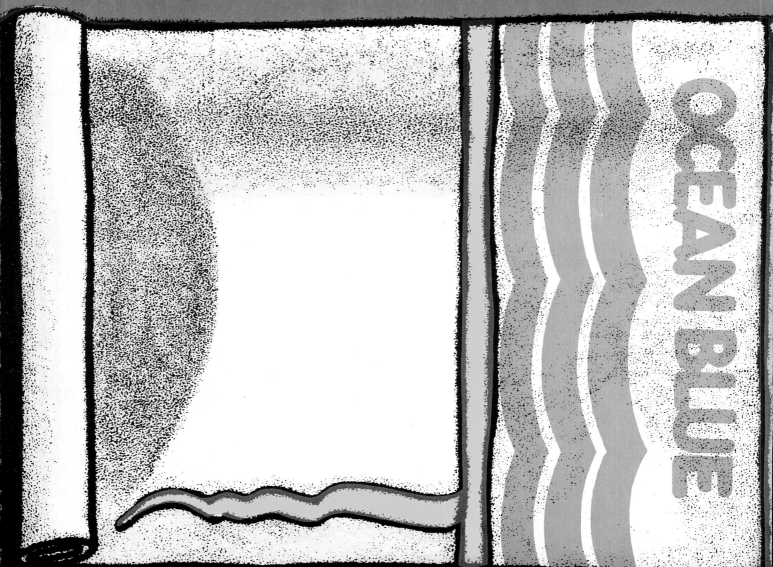

OCEAN BLUE

together his supplies to spend a weekend at the
seashore, sketching
pictures for the
Fall Festival of Art.

Before leaving   he gave each of his

children some paper to use while he was away.

Now while he was gone,
one child who had received five sheets
of paper began to make five colorful paintings.

The second child who had received
two sheets of paper began to
make two crayon drawings.

But the third child, who had received one piece of pape

went to his room, alone.

There he hid his paper under the bed.

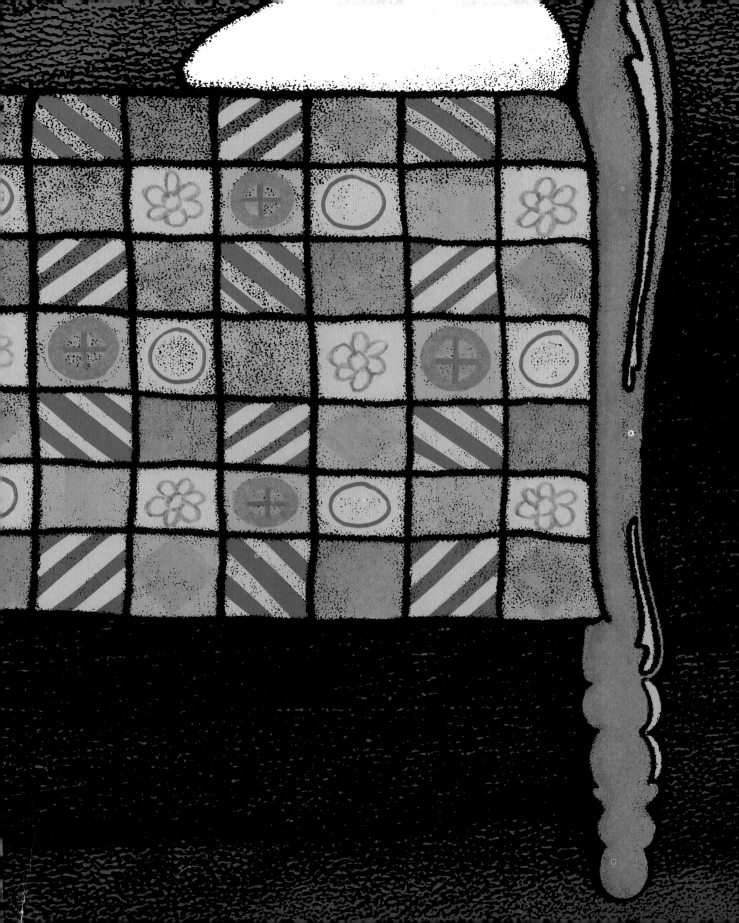

After a few days, the famous artist retu

...ed home with a large bundle of sketches.

"How bright .... how soft ....

how large............how happy, how grand!" he said.

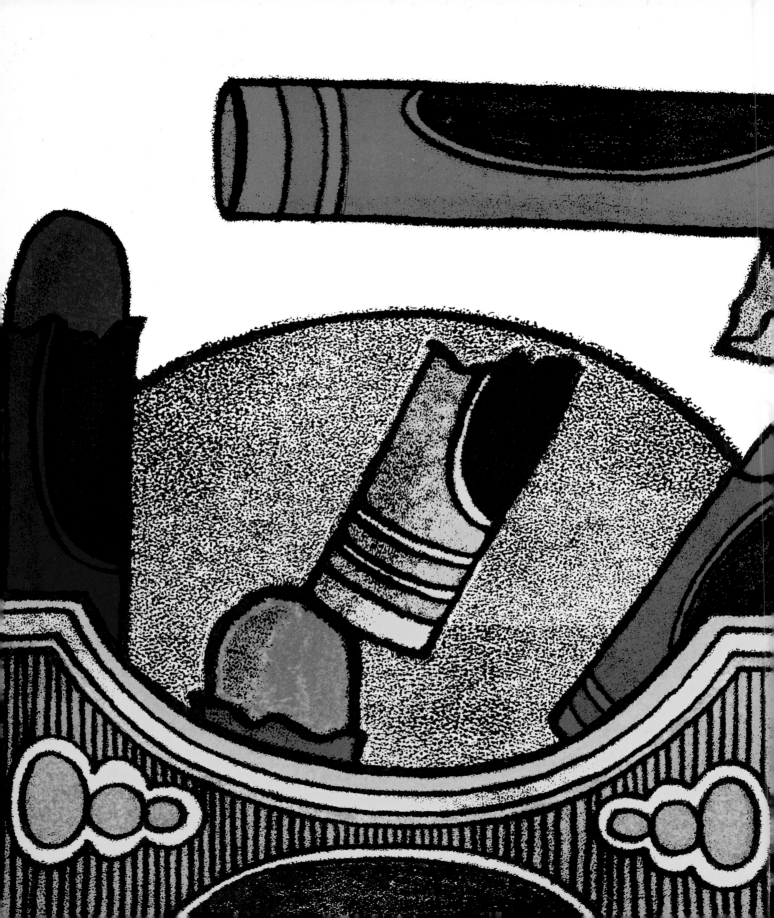

Then his second child came running.
She too, was excited about what she had to
show. "Look what I made, Father!"
she said. "Two drawings!"

"How graceful, how clever!" he said. He was very

pleased. He was so pleased that he said,

"How would you
like to hang your
pictures with mine
at the Festival of Art!"
His children could hardly
believe their ears.
"Yes! Yes!" they shouted.

Just then the third child came, but he wasn't running

"Father," he said, "I was so afraid I would make a mistake that I didn't do anything."

"Here is the paper you gave me," he said with a blank stare. "Do you mean you wouldn't even try?" his father asked.

"Wouldn't that be a mistake not to try?
Let's make a picture now so that you will have
something to show at the Festival of Art."

So the child made the best picture he could make.

And when all of
their pictures were hung at the Festival of Art

people gathered around them in small groups.

Everyone said it was the artist's finest exhibit.